MW01620684

Starting The Journey

A 30 day Devotional

Pursuing Christ Ministries Devotional Series
Book 1

Tamala May

Copyright © 2023 by Tamala May

All rights reserved

Printed in the United States of America

Print ISBN: 978-1-952385-82-7

eBook ISBN:978-1-952385-81-0

Cover Designed by: Tammy Mowrey and Above The Sun LLC

Scripture quotations marked (NLT) are taken from the *Holy Bible*, New Living Translation, copyright © 1996, 2004, 2015 by Tyndale House Foundation. Used by permission of Tyndale House Publishers, Carol Stream, Illinois 60188, USA. All rights reserved.

Scripture quotations marked (NIV) are taken from the Holy Bible, New International Version®, NIV®. Copyright © 1973, 1978, 1984, 2011 by Biblica, Inc.™ Used by permission of Zondervan. All rights reserved worldwide. www.zondervan.comThe "NIV" and "New International Version" are trademarks registered in the United States Patent and Trademark Office by Biblica, Inc.™

Scripture quotations marked ESV are from The ESV® Bible (The Holy Bible, English Standard Version®), copyright © 2001 by Crossway, a publishing ministry of Good News Publishers. Used by permission. All rights reserved.

This book has been produced in association with Above The Sun, LLC who has a mission to help authors release heaven through their authentic stories. For author coaching or publishing advice, visit: https://abovethesun.org

No portion of this book may be reproduced or transmitted in any form or by any means—electronic, mechanical, photocopy, recording, scanning, or other—except for brief quotations without the express written permission of the author.

Contents

Introduction vii

1. He's Calling 1
2. Faith Versus Knowledge 4
3. Beyond Battles 6
4. Fire Acceleration 9
5. Speak Up 12
6. Know Your Beauty 15
7. Lingering Bitterness 18
8. The Ever-Popular Selfie 20
9. Fear Not 22
10. I'm Sorry 25
11. Christian Stock Market 28
12. The Desires of the Heart 31
13. Impossibility 34
14. Second Look 38
15. Watering and Fertilizing Thoughts 41
16. Seeking Wisdom 44
17. Do It My Way 47
18. MVP Player 50
19. Hand Hygiene 53
20. Let Freedom Ring 55
21. Great Opportunities 58
22. Limitless 61
23. Bible Meditation 64
24. Matter of Perspective 67
25. Church Etiquette 69
26. Holistic Spirituality 72
27. Auditory Assessment 75
28. Amputation Option 78

29. Where's Your Shield 81
30. Death Departure 84

Prayer of Salvation 87
About The Author 89
Other Books By Tamala May 91

This book is dedicated to those friends that helped me grow in my faith and were persistent in keeping me on this journey to publish. This book would not have been possible without all of you.

Introduction

Being in this world can be hard, and we all need a Savior. As Christians, we are on a continuous lifelong journey to build and sustain our faith. It is essential for each of us to connect daily with the Lord. We are prone to stray and wander away when we are not purposeful in our faith journey. Devotional messages are one resource that can powerfully affect our walk with the Lord.

If you are not a Christian yet, may these messages help you to understand who God is, the amazing love He has for us, and His gracious benefits. May these thought-provoking words encourage you to make the best choice of your life.

After I reached a very difficult place in my life, pursuing Christ became essential to my ability to face and overcome the challenges I encountered. During this time, Christian inspirations and words offered me much-needed encouragement. As I drew closer to the Lord, I discovered an anointing to write messages of encouragement that were given to me from the Lord. These messages have been shared with friends and family, who found them impactful in their lives and who encouraged me to publish these messages so others could also be inspired.

In this book, you will find thirty of these devotionals to help enrich your life and faith journey. They have been designed to give you a start or boost in your journey of pursuing the Lord. In our busy world, these short daily devotions provide meaningful messages that are quick and easy to read.

These messages are written to encourage and inspire adults and older teens who are looking for additional ways to build their faith. The devotions include such topics as staying strong in your spiritual battle, forgiveness, hearing God, identifying your calling, reflecting on your personal faith, and building a stronger faith walk. These messages will help individuals who are beginning their faith journey, who are at a difficult time in their life, or who are striving to advance their faith. These messages will empower believers as they encourage self-reflection based on words and ideas from scripture.

As you read these devotionals may you grow in your faith journey. May you become a stronger Christian that you might be a lighthouse and encouragement to others. In deepening your faith, may you find your anointing and the calling the Lord has specifically for you in your life. As you continue pursuing Christ, may you find a deeper love for the Lord, granting you an inexplicable peace and joy that can only come from Him.

Chapter 1

He's Calling

Each of you should continue to live in whatever situation the Lord has placed you, and remain as you were when God first called you. This is my rule for all the churches.
1 Corinthians 7:17 (NLT)

Our thoughts and emotions originate and are stored in the brain. Sometimes when people are overwhelmed with lots of thoughts and emotions at one time, they will say they are "being (or getting) in their head." This refers to being emerged in thoughts of all sorts, which may fluctuate across an entire spectrum from Godly to driven by flesh and Satan. The initial surge of thoughts about something can be very different from our final thoughts. Our thoughts can be influenced by our emotions and many other things. Influences can range from our heritage, culture, faith, circumstances, people we are surrounded by, and many more things. Understanding what is happening with our thoughts and what is driving these thoughts is a great value in understanding and interpreting the effects they have on the words we speak and our faith.

When Moses first encountered God and was given his assignment, "Moses pleaded with the Lord, 'Oh Lord, I'm not very good with words. I never have been, and I'm not now, even though you have spoken to me. I get tongue-tied, and my words get tangled'" (Exodus 4:10 NLT). His thoughts were driven by his emotions. Moses was given a great task, which certainly seemed overwhelming. His response was to belittle himself and his ability to do the work God was calling him to do.

Gideon was also called by God. Judges 6:11-27 recounts when the angel of the Lord came down to speak to Gideon. Israel had fallen into the hands of the Midianites for seven years, and now God was sending Gideon to reclaim Israel. When first approached by the angel of the Lord in Verse 13, "And Gideon said to him, 'Please, my Lord, if the LORD is with us, why then has all of this happened to us? And where are all his wonderful deeds that our fathers recounted to us saying, 'Did not the LORD bring us up from Egypt?' But now the LORD has forsaken us and given us into the hand of the Midian"(ESV). Gideon's words displayed his emotions along with his thoughts of insecurity and lack of self-confidence.

Another example of an emotional response in the New Testament occurs when Zechariah is called by the Lord. In Luke 1:13, Zechariah was told by an angel of the Lord that Sarah, who was old in age, would become pregnant. "Zechariah asked the angel, 'How can I be sure of this? I am an old man and my wife is well along in years'" (v. 18 NIV). Zechariah's words were littered with doubt of the impossible and unbelief in the power of the Lord.

Other scriptures display thoughts in a very different manner. In Genesis 6, we read of the response of Noah after finding favor in God's eyes and being given very detailed instructions about building an ark. He did not respond verbally, but in Verse 22, it says, "Noah did everything just as God commanded him" (NIV).

When Jesus called His disciples to drop their nets and follow Him, there was never any documented resistance—they just went. In Luke 1:38, after the angel told Mary that she, a virgin, would bear a son, the Savior, "Mary responded, 'I am the Lord's servant. May everything you have said about me come true.' and then the angel left her." (NLT). In these examples we see those whose thoughts were led by faith and not by their human emotions.

Today, I encourage you to think about something you feel God is calling you to do. Ask yourself if you are receptive to this, or are your first thoughts of resistance, fear, or lack of confidence? The good news is that regardless of your initial response, if God is calling you to do something, He will equip you and provide the way and means for you to complete that calling. While Moses, Gideon, and Zechariah all had initial thoughts that were not receptive, God still facilitated a way for them to do the assignment He had designed for them, and He will do the same for you. There will always be many types of thoughts in your brain, many driven by emotions. You are not alone in the process of sifting through your thoughts. But today, may you have faith to "take captive every thought to make it obedient to Christ" (2 Corinthians 10:5 NIV). With thoughts that are obedient to God's will, your steps in walking out your calling will be designed by the Lord. There will be no place for insecurity, shame, unworthiness, or lack of faith. Today may you be receptive to Him and anticipate with excitement the call He has for you.

Chapter 2

Faith Versus Knowledge

Then I saw all that God has done. No one comprehends what goes on under the sun. Despite all their efforts to search it out, no one can discover its meaning. Even if the wise claim they know, they cannot really comprehend it.

Ecclesiastes 8:17 (NIV)

Vision allows us to see physical things. However, vision can also be used to describe being able to see a plan, dream, or strategy that is not physically visible.

Years ago, I was working as a nurse in a Heart Failure Clinic. The research and technology for how to treat these patients was changing rapidly, and we were finding the program beginning to have great potential for tremendous rapid growth. Because of this, we needed a strategic plan to set out a process for growing the program. We needed to determine long and short-term goals. As workers in the clinic, we were the ones assigned to do this since we knew the disease, innovations, and the patients' needs. We knew the business, so we could see the vision.

We also need vision when it comes to our spiritual journey. The more we know and understand the Lord and what His Word says, the more clearly we can see the Lord. The stronger our faith becomes, the clearer and better our vision becomes. First John 4:12-13 says, "No one has ever seen God; but if we love one another, God lives in us and his love is made complete in us. This is how we know that we live in him and he in us; He has given us his Spirit" (NIV).

As we strengthen our faith, God and His power, majesty, and love for us come into plain view. When we begin to see God's work all around us, our faith then becomes reality. Romans 1:20 says, "For since the creation of the world God's invisible qualities—his eternal power and divine nature—have been clearly seen, being understood from what has been made, so that people are without excuse" (NIV).

God has a vision for each one of us. He has a plan to shape us and develop us. Isaiah 64:8 says, "But now, O Lord, you are our Father; we are the clay, and you are the potter, we are all the work of your hand"(ESV). For God to create the vision He has for each of us, we must grow closer to Him and submit to Him so that His work may be accomplished in our lives. Philippians 2:13 says, "For God is working in you, giving you the desire and the power to do what pleases him" (NLT).

Today may you allow the master visionary to be at work in your life developing the child He desires you to be and demonstrating His purpose for your life. You may not see or know the strategic plan of the Lord, but He created it before you were born and will see it through if you allow Him.

Chapter 3

Beyond Battles

What shall we say about such wonderful things as these? If God is for us, who can ever be against us?
Romans 8:31 (NLT)

When the youngest of my three children graduated from high school, I remember having tears in my eyes. There were some tears about my daughter beginning a new chapter and me having an empty nest, but the most tears were because we made it. I had become a single mom when my oldest was a junior in high school, and the road to getting all three of my children graduated alone was difficult and at times seemed nearly impossible. This battle seemed enormous. All I had known was parenting with their father, and doing it alone seemed more than I could imagine. I know now the only reason I made it through without many permanent battle wounds was because God was there helping me fight that battle.

We all face battles of many kinds. Sometimes we can feel like the battles of this world are big and we are under-prepared or ill-equipped. In scripture, we see the Philistines, the enemy of the Israelites, challenge to send their toughest warrior against the toughest warrior of the Israelites to settle their dispute. David's brothers, who were all soldiers and older than he was, were propositioned to take on this challenge, but none of them would. David was a shepherd boy without any military experience, but when he heard Goliath mocking Israel and their God, he stepped forward to take on the giant. There is some discrepancy in literature, but Goliath was very tall—with estimates ranging from seven to nine feet tall, while David was estimated to be around five feet. David tried to put on the warrior gear of King Saul, but it was far too big and clumsy for him. He was offered the best of the best in armor but did not use it. He decided to go without any gear and chose five smooth stones and a sling as his weapon. David defeated this giant with just one of the stones.

David was able to defeat Goliath because of the faith he had in the God he served—not by any skill or ability he had on his own. David was entering into a warrior's battle with rocks and a sling. Sometimes in this world we feel like David, totally unprepared and ill equipped for the battles we face. Sometimes we feel like we are bringing rocks to a sword fight.

When we face battles that are bigger than we are, we need to learn from David and trust in the Lord. Exodus 14:14 says, "The Lord himself will fight for you; you need only to be still" (NIV). When we see these giants in our lives, it can induce worry and anxiety, manifesting itself in many negative ways in our lives. Then God says, "Stay calm; trust me, I've got this for you." Deuteronomy 20:4 says, "For the Lord your God is the one who goes with you to fight for you against your enemies to give you victory" (NIV). And Jeremiah 1:19 says, "They will fight against you but will not overcome you, for I am with you and will rescue you,' declares the LORD" (NIV).

Today I encourage you that if your battle feels gigantic, and bigger than you, remember the words of our Father assuring us He is going before and beside us and will rescue us. May you search yourself and have the confidence of David knowing God will defeat your enemy despite feeling like you're inadequate and unprepared. God has promised that He will always be our champion of any battle!

Chapter 4

Fire Acceleration

Seek the Lord and his strength; seek his presence continually!
1 Chronicles 16:11 (ESV)

My sons participated in Boy Scouts when they were growing up and did a lot of campouts. One of their favorite things about camping was the bonfire at the end of the day. They loved building the fire and getting it started. Then they would attentively add wood to keep the fire burning. Sometimes, they would pile too much wood and the flames would burn higher than they should. Other times they would have to stoke the fire to keep it going. They would poke around in the fire to try to get the sparks to ignite a bigger fire.

There is a fire we need to have burning for the Lord within each of us. Just like a campfire, a fire for the Lord requires continual refueling. The fire cannot burn without additives. We are in control of what and how much is added to have a strong fire. There are many accelerants for that fire. The

Church can be a good place to stoke your fire. It can provide an opportunity for refreshing and refueling. There is a natural euphoria that can be experienced when you are worshiping the Lord in the presence of other believers. Any time spent in the Lord's presence, whether meditating on him, reading the Word, praying, or fellowshipping with other believers can be accelerants to your fire. First Thessalonians 5:11 tells us, "So encourage each other and build each other up, just as you are already doing" (NLT).

Being a Christian is an ongoing daily responsibility. Simply declaring your faith and desiring to have a strong faith is not enough. Unfortunately, it is never that easy because the world we live in is occupied by the enemy. The enemy will bring sidetracking circumstances and draining circumstances to distract you from your faith journey. Sometimes the enemy will coerce you to get caught up in distracting things. These things are not necessarily bad and may even seem good, but they take away your time with the Lord.

It is important to always ensure time with God daily so we can stay fueled up and strong in our faith. God reminds us of this continual process in Philippians 2:12: "Dear friend, you always followed my instructions when I was with you. And now that I am away, it is even more important. Work hard to show the results of your salvation, obeying God with deep reverence and fear" (NLT). In the process of investing this time, we will find ourselves maturing in our faith. First Peter 2:2 describes it, saying, "Like newborn babies, you must crave pure spiritual milk so that you will grow into a full experience of salvation. Cry out for this nourishment" (NLT). As we satisfy and build our faith with the spiritual milk, we will see it strengthen and a fire for the Lord grow.

Today if you feel like there is not a burning fire of faith in you, I encourage you to get some accelerant on that fire and make it burn. Unlike sometimes when you try to start a fire and the conditions are less than ideal, with faith the fire always has perfect conditions and will be guaranteed to heat up when you feed it. Today don't be a smoldering Christian; be one that burns red hot!

Chapter 5

Speak Up

For it will not be you speaking, but the Spirit of your Father speaking through you.
Matthew 10:20 (NIV)

One superstition in healthcare is never saying "it's quiet" when things are not busy. This belief is to the extent that people will use all sorts of other words or phrases to comment on a slow day to avoid actually saying the word quiet. Saying the word quiet was thought to surely bring a very busy time.

There is a taboo ritual in this world that some people hold, where they are afraid if they speak something it might happen. They might say things like "I'm not going to say that out loud or it might come true" or they may say "if I say it then I'll just jinx myself." It's like we all have this knowledge of the power of speaking specific words or messages and the resulting outcomes of those spoken words. Yet it is not uncommon to read God's word and know it but fail to speak it into situations in our lives. When we know and understand God's word and do not speak it into our situation or apply it to our lives, we really are only using a portion of the power within the word God has given to us.

There are many self-help books, videos, and lessons describing the power of the spoken word. The effect of the spoken word has become fundamental to many self-help therapies. The Bible also tells us the importance of the spoken word and we see examples throughout scripture. The first example we see in scripture is as the world is being formed. The third verse of the entire Bible says in Genesis 1:3, "And God said, 'Let there be light,' and there was light"(NIV). Genesis 1 continues and describes how God spoke to the waters to separate and there to be a sky, he commended the lands to produce vegetation and living creatures to be made. Throughout the entire chapter over and over God speaks and the world and creation responded to his words.

The spoken power of God's word is mighty! Understanding the word of God and not speaking it will prevent us from having the full extent of the power God has granted us. It is in speaking out loud the word of God that another level of power is released greater than any other times. Jeremiah 23:28 says, "Let the one who has my word speak it faithfully . . ." (NIV) and Verse 29 says, "Is not my word like fire,' declares the Lord,'and like a hammer that breaks a rock in many pieces" (NIV). And Isaiah 55:11 says, "so is my word that comes out from my mouth: It will not return to me empty, but will accomplish what I desire and achieve the purpose for which I sent it" (NIV).

When we are faced with difficult situations, speaking the word of God will create a fire and power that can come only from God. We may have apprehension about speaking out loud the word of God because we believe reading it and understanding it is enough. However, when we use the words the

Lord has given us, the power exponentially increases. The enemy understands the power of the spoken word, and he does not want that power released. He will use hesitation and intimidation in our minds when we are about to speak God's word to prevent a release of godly power.

Today I encourage you to speak the word of God, shout it from the mountaintops, release power that is far beyond any power you ever imagined. This spoken word has the ability to change your life and those around you who hear those words.

Do not keep the word of God silent and inside. It is the power of the spoken word that created the world and offers you tremendous power in your life and circumstances. Speak the word of God boldly that His word may achieve its purpose and shatter rocks and start fires. Use the whole power of God that you have been granted, and watch what He does.

Chapter 6

Know Your Beauty

Know that the Lord is God. It is he who made us, and we are his; we are his people, the sheep of his pasture.
Psalm 100:3 (NIV)

Anorexia nervosa is an eating disorder characterized by abnormally low body weight and intense fear of gaining weight. Individuals with this condition will go to grave lengths to maintain this low body weight, including not eating for long periods of time, excessive exercise, and vomiting of food. While this is an eating disorder, it is more about how people perceive themselves than what goes on with food and digestion. Individuals suffering from this disorder can only see themselves as fat despite being extremely thin even to the point of cachexia and being dangerously unhealthy. We can look at them and see how horribly thin and ill they appear, but they cannot see that in themselves. The only thing they see is the consuming vision of being fat and unhappy about their appearance.

Sometimes we approach God with a distorted view of

ourselves. We see ourselves as inadequate, unworthy, a failure, ugly, alienated, ashamed, betrayed, screwed up, stupid, an outcast, left out, hopeless, dirty, a disappointment, humiliated, etc. The list is endless. We have convinced ourselves that we are all of those things, but God sees who we really are and calls us His precious children that He created and chose. First John 3:1 says, "See how much our Father has loved us, for He calls us his children, and that is what we are! But the people who belong to this world don't recognize that we are God's children because they don't know him" (NLT). It is the world that tells us we are all the negative things we see in ourselves, but it is not what God sees or tells us we are. When we believe what the world tells us, we are criticizing what God created.

A unique thing about parents is regardless of what a child may look like or be, parents find beauty in their own child. If you look on social media, you will see children with birth defects and deformities posted all the time with inscriptions about the joy and blessing that child has brought and the beauty they see in their child regardless of the outward appearance. No matter what a child looks like, each parent will see the beauty, worth, and special qualities of each child and hope for great things in the child's life. God sees us, His children, this way too.

As Christians, we can be confident in how our Father in heaven sees us. He sees us as His precious creation. Psalm 139:14 says, "I praise you because I am fearfully and wonderfully made; your works are wonderful, I know that full well" (NIV). Isaiah 64:8 also says, "But now, O Lord, You are our Father, we are the clay, and you are our potter; we are all the work of your hand" (ESV). God doesn't make things that are ugly, failures or unworthy. He is an amazing God that only makes amazing things.

Today look at yourself, and if you have misconceptions

about the imperfections and faults you see in yourself, like the anorexic not seeing their thin bodies, I challenge you to try looking at yourself as the Creator does and see who you really are. See what the enemy tries to tell you falsely that you are, and recognize the truth of the wonderful thing you are because you were made by God. The world may not recognize those things in you, but God always will.

Chapter 7

Lingering Bitterness

Get rid of all bitterness, rage, anger, harsh words, and slander, as well as all types of evil behavior.
Ephesians 4:31 (NLT)

In grade school we learned the tongue is the part of the body allowing us to experience the sense of taste, both pleasurable and unpleasurable. The tongue has different zones that allow us to experience these different tastes. The front of the tongue is where we experience sweetness, and the sides toward the front are where we taste salty. Both of these tastes are desirable, and people crave these tastes. But the back of the tongue, toward the base deep in the mouth, is where we experience the taste of bitterness. Bitterness is a taste no one desires and is a flavor that tends to linger with you. Sometimes people will comment, "I just can't get that out of my mouth."

Bitterness can exist in our lives because of things we experience. Just like a bitter taste can be hard to get rid of, the bitterness in our lives can also linger. This continued bitterness can have a negative effect on our lives if we do not rid ourselves of it. Bitterness can be related to anger, disappointment, or inequality. Acts 8:23 says, "For I see that you are full of bitterness and captive to sin" (NIV). Proverbs 14:10 says, "Each heart knows its own bitterness, and no one else can share its joy" (NIV). Bitterness can continue to affect us long after the event that caused the bitterness. The longer that bitterness remains, the harder it often is to get rid of it.

Bad experiences that make us bitter can include disagreements or a conversation with someone saying things that are hurtful. Maybe someone cheated you out of some money or property. Maybe someone lied to you, or maybe they misled you and caused you to make a bad decision.

Bitterness is removed when we are able to forgive and release the feelings keeping us captive to it. Hebrews 12:14-15 tells us, "Work at living in peace with everyone, and work at living a holy life, for those who are not holy will not see the Lord. Look after each other so that none of you fails to receive the grace of God. Watch out that no poisonous root of bitterness grows up to trouble you, corrupting many" (NLT).

Today may you identify any bitterness in your life and allow God to help you remove it. Our flesh may hold us captive to bitterness, but through the Lord, we are able to overcome it. Then we can once again fully enjoy all the sweetness and desirable tastes of life.

Chapter 8

The Ever-Popular Selfie

Turn my eyes away from worthless things; preserve my life according to your word.
Psalm 119:37 (NIV)

Years ago, most of us would never have fathomed holding a computer with its many functions in our hands. A friend told me there were predictions that someday people would walk around with handheld computers. Welcome to the twenty-first century and the advent of the cell phone—a device that has the ability to do amazing things at the touch of a finger. The era of the cell phone and its ability to take photos has, for the most part, eliminated handheld cameras. The days of mailing in film and waiting weeks for the pictures to return are long gone. However, with the advent of the cell phone, the "selfie" has become part of our daily lives. Today, selfies have become the essence of social media. People post images of how they want the world to see them.

Unfortunately, what the selfie can truly show is how self-focused we have become. We can become occupied with ourselves. While a selfie on its own is not a bad thing, we must be able to recognize when our focus becomes more on ourselves than on God and when we spend more time with the lens turned on ourselves than on God. Colossians 3:1 says, "Since, then, you have been raised with Christ, set your eyes on things above, where Christ is, seated at the right hand of God" (NIV). Keeping our eyes focused on godly things can be difficult. As earthly beings we are easily distracted, and focusing on ourselves can be like a reflex, something that happens without intent or thought. Circumstances in our lives and challenging times can cause us to focus our eyes inward very readily. Recognizing the reflex we have to focus inward will allow us to be more diligent in making sure that we focus upward instead.

The benefits of being focused on God include seeing Him more clearly and understanding and believing in Him at new depths. Being focused on God will bring increased awareness and fruitfulness to our life. In John 15:4, Jesus says, "Remain in me, as I also remain in you. No branch can bear fruit by itself; it must remain in the vine. Neither can you bear fruit unless you remain in me" (NIV). Isaiah 26:3 says, "You keep him in perfect peace whose mind is stayed on you, because he trusts in you" (ESV).

We must all challenge ourselves in this century to determine where our focus lies. It is easy to become "selfie" focused. The beauty in our focus comes when it is not on us but on God. When we do this, we will see glimpses of God and His work woven throughout our lives, bringing us joy, peace, and strength. The benefits from a life focused on God are immeasurable and filled with promises from God that will never disappoint.

Chapter 9

Fear Not

Don't be afraid, for I am with you. Don't be discouraged, for I am your God. I will strengthen you and help you. I will hold you up with my victorious right hand.
Isaiah 41:10 (NLT)

Experiencing fear happens to all of us at one time or another and can bring strife and discord to our lives. Fear of financial disaster, losing a child, a bad health diagnosis, a marriage in distress, family members with dependency problems, and the list goes on. Christians profess God's faithfulness during these times, which is what we want to believe. Yet, as we watch things around us, it can become difficult to believe. Things may continue to go wrong, and we wonder how God could possibly be working in all of it. The fear in these situations can become consuming, robbing us of our faith in God and our peace.

After graduating from grad school with my master's as a nurse practitioner, I had a waiting period between taking my licensing examination and starting work. I decided this was a good time to get my annual physical examination and medical prevention screening appointments done. My mammogram revealed an abnormality, leading to additional diagnostic testing and possibly facing a cancer diagnosis. This additional testing confirmed the abnormality, which led to a breast biopsy. In addition, my husband had just left me and my three children. I was gripped with fear of possible cancer, a divorce, financial disaster, and raising three children alone.

What if I had cancer? How was I going to support my family? How was I going to be able to do treatments and continue to work? I only had two months remaining on my current health insurance since I was between jobs. What if my insurance ran out? How was I going to pay for cancer care? What if I didn't pass my licensing exam? The list of "what ifs" ran through my head almost continually.

I'm happy to report that the breast biopsy was negative and all the "what ifs" that I was worrying about were a waste of time and energy. Had I just trusted the Lord, I could have saved myself from so much worry and fear.

In scripture, the story of Joshua is a perfect example of overcoming fear. After Moses died, Joshua was given the assignment by God to lead the Israelite people into the promised land. The nation of Israel had followed Moses for forty years in the wilderness after God delivered them from slavery, provided them a safe escape, and cared for their needs. Now Moses had passed and Joshua was commissioned to lead the Israelites into the Promised Land. The army he was leading was thought to be about 600,000 men, and with women and children there was a total of around two million people. Joshua, being one of the original spies to survey the land, had seen the Promised Land and knew the inhabitants were mighty and going against them would be no small task. Joshua's fear must have been intense because he was told to be "strong and courageous" four times—three times by God and once by God's people. Three more times Joshua was told that God was with him. He likely needed the repeated reassurance because of the intensity of his fear. Because God was with Joshua, he was able to successfully lead the people into the Promised Land and conquer the land.

We are often like Joshua when facing fear, needing to be reminded regularly that God will be with us wherever we go. Throughout scripture, God promises to be with His people in difficult situations as they obey and put their trust in Him. He will do the same for us. When we transfer our fear into hope, we are freed from the torment and toil of fear.

So today if your fear is rampant, know the Lord your God is with you. God gave us the Bible as an instruction manual and way to know Him better. His Word assures us that when life is tough or the assignment is great, He will always be there. When God our Father is with us, there is no room for fear despite any obstacles the enemy tries to create. Fear is a strategy of the enemy, and hope is the promise of God. Choose wisely which you let manifest in your life.

Chapter 10

I'm Sorry

Yes, each of us will give a personal account to God.
Romans 14:12 (NLV)

I recall a situation I did not handle right and someone confronting me about it afterwards. While I knew they were right, my instinctive response was to say, "Well, I did it because they said some things that were hurtful" or "I wouldn't have done that if they would not have treated me the way they did." Many of us can admit to having these responses at some time or another when we have been corrected and are faced with apologizing about something.

It is difficult to hear and challenging to stay positive when we are shown that we did something wrong. Being commanded to be Christlike, we ought to reflect on His responses and behavior. He did not hang on a cross and accuse people of the wrong they had done to him. Instead, He was gracious, loving, and forgiving. First John 2:6 says, "Whoever claims to live in him must live as Jesus did"(NIV). He was full of kindness to those who treated him wrong and was free of any condemnation.

Certainly, my situation was not a big deal, but it was enough to irritate me when I was corrected. After days of considering multiple ways to justify how I had behaved, I decided it was time to take ownership of my mistakes. I went to the person who had corrected me and apologized for mishandling the situation. They forgave me, and I had a great sense of relief. When we are able to humble ourselves, we can find great peace in the acknowledgment of our wrongdoing.

Being a Christian is not about looking for reasons to justify our wrongdoings. It is about acknowledging them, asking for forgiveness, and pressing forward to make ourselves more Christlike. John 3:30 says, "He must become greater and greater; and I must become less and less" (NLV). So today if there are things that you know you have not handled well, go back and correct them. Own your misdeeds. Withhold any accusations of what the other person or persons may have done to provoke you to behave in the manner you did. A sincere apology is about acceptance of what we did regardless of the other person's actions. Our responsibility is to us and our actions, and their responsibility is to theirs. We will all stand before the throne on judgment day and should desire to have a clear conscience, not one tainted by failure to own our misgivings and mistakes.

Once we have apologized and repented to the Lord, we can release the situation. Carrying guilt and bad feelings about the situation after repentance is a burden the Lord never intended for us to bear. But our enemy, the devil, wants us to continue to carry it all. He does not want us to experience the freedom and renewal granted in repentance. Releasing those feelings is sometimes even harder than the act of repentance and apologizing. Colossians 2:13-14 says, "You were dead because of your sins and because your sinful nature was not yet cut away. Then God made you alive with Christ, for he forgave all our sins. He canceled the record of the charges against us and took it away by nailing it to the cross" (NLT). Acts 3:19 says, "Repent, then, and turn to God, so that your sins may be wiped out, that times of refreshing may come from the Lord"(NIV). Accept the gift of grace from God and be renewed. We no longer have to be tied to the ugly emotions associated with our mistakes. God has given us the ability to blot those things out, and once they are gone there ought to be no residue of them in our life. Saying we are sorry is something all of us have to do from time to time because of our sinful nature. But God understands and offers us the grace we need to allow us to forgive ourselves.

Chapter 11

Christian Stock Market

Give generously to them and do so without a grudging heart; then because of this the LORD your God will bless you in all your work and in everything you put your hand to.
Deuteronomy 15:10 (NIV)

When I got my first job with real benefits, I was introduced to the idea of a 401K and matching contributions. It seemed kind of out of reach to plan for retirement when I was so young, but I quickly learned how saving at a young age could multiply my earnings and cause them to grow exponentially over the years. When you are investing, there is always an option to be riskier with your investments in hopes that you will have larger gains or to be conservative with lower, more guaranteed gains. The big earnings are tempting, but there is always the risk of big losses associated with them. For some, being in risky investments can be very stressful as they may watch their money grow rapidly and at times drop rapidly.

As Christians, we invest in our faith. Unlike financial

investments, when we invest in the Lord, we are guaranteed a great return. An investment in the Lord does not mean saving and conserving our money. It means giving of our time, money, and gifts. In this reverse investment, you can see guaranteed great returns from the Lord. When we invest financially, we are working to save and build reserve funds, but with the Lord, we must pour out and give without knowing what or how the return will come. However, God does assure us there will be a return on our giving.

Scripture repeatedly tells us about the returns we will receive when we give in the name of the Lord. Luke 6:38 says, "Give, and you will receive. Your gift will return to you in full—pressed down, shaken together to make room for more, running over, and poured into your lap. The amount you give will determine the amount you get back" (NLT). Proverbs 11:24-25 says, "Give freely and become more wealthy; be stingy and lose everything. The generous will prosper; those who refresh others will themselves be refreshed" (NLT). Second Corinthians 9:6 says, "The point is this: whoever sows sparingly will also repeat sparingly, and whoever sows bountifully will reap bountifully" (ESV).

After my husband left me, I was in the worst financial position I have ever been in. I had more money going out each month than I had coming in and had a huge debt load. This created a tremendous amount of anxiety, stress, and worry. However, this was a pivotal point in growing my faith, and I knew what the Word said about tithing and being generous, so I started to tithe. Honestly, there were times when I was writing my check and I questioned if I should be doing it since money was so tight. I had struggled with so many other aspects of my life and decided if I could trust God with everything else in my life, I could trust him with my money too. In a few short years, my financial status was better than it had ever been in my entire life, and I credit it all to the Lord.

When we invest our time and money into the things He has called us to, there is no risk in this kind of investment. Furthering the kingdom of God does not require any formula to determine our gains. When you invest in Christ and the kingdom of heaven, our rewards will increase. The more we invest, the greater the return. We do have to wait for our retirement gains, but God will begin blessing us right away when we begin investing in Him. These gains and blessings may not be financial, but they will likely be gains that are far more valuable than anything money could buy. There will never be a loss because of the guarantee our Father has given us. So today, go invest. Invest significantly and boldly. We cannot lose a thing. God has assured us there will be a great return on our investment in Him every time.

Chapter 12

The Desires of the Heart

Wherever your treasure is, there the desires of your heart will also be.
Matthew 6:21 (NLT)

As children go through grade school and high school, they frequently are asked, "What do you want to be when you grow up?" For some that is an easy question, but others struggle to figure out what profession they want to pursue. I'm in the group that always knew what they wanted to do. It's also not uncommon to hear adults voice regrets about things they had wanted to do in their lives but because of circumstances they were prevented from ever doing them.

In college, I attended my first Christian concert. In the middle, the artist took a break to give a message about how God would give you the desire in your heart for what He wants you to do. He said God wouldn't call you to the mission field in another country if that wasn't something you had a desire to do. He gives you a heart and passion for the things He is calling you to do.

In my second semester at college, I had gotten pretty comfortable being away from home and had made lots of friends. I began to get very active in my social life. Needless to say, this was not compatible with study habits. That particular semester I was taking eighteen credits, nine of which were science, which meant a lot of studying. I failed my first tests in chemistry, anatomy, and anatomy lab. These were hard classes to get passing grades without starting out with failing grades. This put me in a position where I would have to do exceptionally well to obtain a passing grade. I was convinced there was no way this could be done, so I pulled out the academic catalog and began to look for another major not requiring these courses.

At that point, I was convinced that my IQ was the problem, not my social habits. Yet, as I looked through the book, I found the only thing I wanted to do was be a nurse. I decided I needed to change my habits and start doing some serious studying. It took hard work and extreme dedication, but I did get through those classes. With changes in my habits and dedication to my courses, I graduated from nursing school without any further difficulty. But I did learn that God gave me the desire to do this job and has equipped me for it. Over the years of nursing, I have seen God move many times and in many ways as I walked out this calling on my life.

No matter what you do in life, if you stay close to God in your walk, then the desires in your heart will be from God. Scripture tells us in Psalm 37:4, "Take delight in the Lord, and he will give you the desires of your heart" (NIV). And when God gives you desires, He will provide a way for them to come to fruition when they align with His purpose. While I used careers as an example, there are many other facets of life that you may have desires. They too are from the Father when you walk close with Him. You may have desires for a family, or to do a specific type of volunteer work or ministry. God is good and puts those desires in your heart, so you may accomplish what He planned for you to do before you were ever born. So today I encourage you to examine the desires of your heart and determine if you are allowing God to work out those desires of your heart in your life. If you are spending time with God and seeking His guidance, He will show you the path to walk to make those desires realities. God wants to fulfill every good and God-given desire of your heart.

Chapter 13

Impossibility

Jesus replied, "What is impossible with man is possible with God."
Luke 18:27 (NIV)

When we face difficulties in our lives, we can be found desperately praying for God to do something in our situation. It's not uncommon that this something we are praying for may border on or is miraculous in nature.

My daughter was born with a congenital heart defect and had to have open heart surgery when she was fifteen to replace a valve. They put in a tissue valve to allow her to have a pregnancy, knowing this would be temporary. Eventually, it would have to be replaced with a mechanical valve, which would prohibit her from having any biological children. In January 2021, she had her routine cardiology follow-up appointment, which revealed her valve was starting to deteriorate. We asked if she would still be able to have children based on how it was functioning. The doctor said she would, but she should do it sooner rather than later. So, instead of waiting to get married till the summer of 2022 (which was the original plan), she had her wedding six months after this visit. Within a few months of getting married she was pregnant. She was a high-risk pregnancy and had to have echocardiograms (ultrasound of the heart) each trimester.

When she had her valve replaced, she had a pressure gradient (a measure of the pressure across her defective valve) of 38 to 40 percent. When she was pregnant, she was told her pressure gradient would likely rise temporarily. Although we knew this, it was stressful to watch the numbers climb. Her echocardiogram during her first trimester revealed a pressure gradient of 11 percent, and in the second trimester it went up to 22 percent. My daughter began to feel a bit anxious seeing that number climb, knowing this pregnancy could be causing damage to her valve. Throughout her pregnancy, there were many individuals and multiple teams praying for her and the baby. Then the third trimester echocardiogram came and the gradient was 8 percent. This medically did not even make sense. She was farther along in pregnancy, and the pressure gradient had dropped by more than half. Today she has a healthy, active little boy, and her heart valve is in better shape than it was before her pregnancy. Truly, a miracle that could only come from God.

In these situations, we really want to believe that God can do the miracle we are praying for and know He has the power to, but doubt works its way into our thoughts. In the first chapter of Luke, we hear the story of Zechariah and Elizabeth. They wanted children desperately and were both good people in God's eyes, but had been unable to become pregnant. As a woman, in Jewish culture in those days, being barren would lead to being shunned and disgraced. Zechariah, who was a priest, had been chosen to enter the sanctuary of the Lord to pray and burn incense. While he prayed and burned incense an angel of the Lord appeared to him and told him Elizabeth would bear a child. The angel went on to tell him what a precious child his son would be and the delight he would bring to men and to God. The angel told Zechariah of the wonderful things this child would do. Zechariah's response was one of questioning. "Zechariah asked the angel, 'How can I be sure of this? I am an old man, and my wife is well along in years." (Luke 1:18 NIV). Then, because Zechariah doubted God, he was unable to speak until after this child was born. God told him, "But now, since you didn't believe what I said, you will be silent and unable to speak until the child is born. For my words will certainly be fulfilled at the proper time" (Luke 1:20 NLT). Zechariah and Elizabeth did have a child, and he would be known as John the Baptist, who would prepare the way for Jesus's coming. This birth was truly a miraculous work of God.

As humans, we desire to have faith that God will do the impossible in our lives and to trust God entirely about this, but we sometimes fall short and give into fear and doubt about whether He will. Jesus encourages us in Mark 11:24, saying, "I tell you, you can pray for anything, and if you believe that you've received it, it will be yours"(NLT). And in Matthew 19:26, it says, "Jesus looked at them (the disciples) and said, 'with man this is impossible, but with God all things are possible'" (NIV). God always works things out even when it requires the impossible, but God tells us that for these things to be granted, we must also believe. When we do our part and believe, we can receive it before it even occurs.

When you see signs of God working out miracles in your life and you feel like God is telling you He will do what looks impossible, how do you respond? Are you a Zechariah, immediately doubting and questioning how that could be or why God would do that for you? Or do you cling to the knowledge of who God is, knowing He can do anything?

Today be very conscientious not to let doubt lead you astray so that you never underestimate the power of what God will do in your life to rescue you and your situation. May you have a faith where you never fail to believe God will answer, no matter how impossible or miraculous the solution may seem. That's our God, the God of the impossible and miraculous.

Chapter 14

Second Look

The Lord will rescue me from every evil attack and will bring me safely to his heavenly kingdom. To him be glory for ever and ever. Amen.
2 Timothy 4:18 (NIV)

In my career as a registered nurse, I worked home care and hospice for a period of time. This required me to be on the road throughout my day visiting different homes and facilities to see patients. My car became my office as I spent most of my days traveling. Between these visits, I would try to manage miscellaneous things associated with my job, including calling the doctor's office, dealing with messages from the office, and figuring out where I was going for the next visit (this was prior to GPS). While I never got into an accident, there were many times I would be at an intersection and would swear I had looked both ways and it was clear. But because of my distractions and the busyness of my day, I would sometimes realize at the last moment there was a car coming that I had not noticed. This was always a startling moment, and I would pause to thank the Lord because of His protection.

Sometimes in our lives, we become so busy with distractions we pay little attention to the world around us. We can miss seeing all sorts of things that could cause us danger. That is why our Father in heaven has assured us that He will protect us. Psalm 34:7 says, "For the angel of the LORD is a guard; he surrounds and defends all who fear him" (NLT). Then Verse 19 says, "The righteous person faces many troubles, but the Lord comes to the rescue each time"(NLT). God rescues us and protects us continually.

Whenever I have one of those near misses, I ponder, "How often does God protect us when we don't even realize it?" While I don't have the answer to that question, I can assure you it's much more than we ever imagined. The story of Elisha, a prophet in the Old Testament chosen by God to call His people to revival, is recorded in 1 and 2 Kings. In 2 Kings 6 we see where the king of Syria was making war against Israel and trying to capture Elisha. In Verse 15 Elisha's servant was in despair as they were surrounded by an enemy army. "When the servant of the man of God got up and went out early the next morning, an army with horses and chariots had surrounded the city. 'Oh no, my Lord! What shall we do?' the servant asked'"(NIV). The prophet assured the servant those who were with him were more than those who were with the enemy. Elisha then asked the Lord to open the eyes of his servant. Verse 17 says, "The Lord opened the young man's eyes, and when he looked up, he saw that the hillside around Elisha was filled with horses and chariots of fire" (NLT). We may never have the privilege Elisha experienced where his eyes were opened to see what was around him and how God was protecting him. But we can be assured God is always providing invisible protection for us just like He did for Elisha's servant.

Together we can look forward to the day when we get to heaven. When our eyes will be opened and we will likely be overwhelmed seeing how many times God protected us while we were totally unaware. Today I encourage you to pray for continued protection daily. We need his protection despite feeling like we are doing the best we can to protect ourselves. God is all-knowing and protects us more than we can possibly imagine.

Chapter 15

Watering and Fertilizing Thoughts

You will keep in perfect peace all who trust in you, all whose thoughts are fixed on you!
Isaiah 26:3 (NLT)

Growing up on the farm meant I saw a lot of crops planted, growing, and harvested. Over the years, farming has become more and more complex. Now, instead of simply putting seed in well-tilled soil and allowing God to water it and watch it grow, there is a science about the right fertilizers, pesticides, and soil nutrients to make the crops grow bigger, thicker, and produce more. You need the right fertilizer and nutrients applied at the right time, in the right strength, on the right crop to get maximal yields. Pesticides are also customized to remove unwanted weeds and grasses that compete for the nutrients and water needed for the crop to grow.

Our minds are a field as well, a field where thoughts can grow. Believers can easily allow the wrong thoughts to take root and then feed into them. For instance, after my husband left me, I had a sense that I was not a good person, I was undesirable, and nobody would ever be with me. I began to believe that I was not worthy enough for anyone. The thoughts were planted by words my husband said to me, but the more I dwelt on them, the more embedded into my mind they became and the more I believed them. When negative thoughts are replayed over and over again in our minds, they become embedded beliefs.

The mind is a powerful part of the body and can become a battleground. Ephesians 6:12 reminds us the battle we are in is not of flesh and blood but is a spiritual one, one that takes place in the mind. We must control this battleground in our minds. The negative thoughts the enemy tries to plant must be uprooted and extinguished like a pesticide that kills the weeds invading the space and robbing the plant of nutrients. Understanding what is getting fed, watered, fertilized, and exterminated in our minds is necessary.

The struggle in our mind can be difficult. When negative thoughts are invading, it can be as real of a struggle as when we can visibly see the enemy and his weapons. This battle may cause us to wonder how it can be won. First and foremost, we must cling to the assurance that God has already won the battle. He understands the difficulty of this and has given us a helper, the Holy Spirit, to reside in us. Spending time in prayer, reading the Word of God, and soaking in His presence provides the best fertilizer and optimal conditions for the right thoughts to be growing. These spiritual disciplines help to keep unwanted thoughts from taking root in our minds and instead growing words rooted in God.

Today I encourage you to be cautious what you grow in your mind and which thoughts you are feeding and encouraging to grow. Thoughts may be persistent and intense, but our God will always be more intense and persistent. While you may think the battlefield going on in your mind may be too intense to overcome, rely on your helper, the Holy Spirit, He is experienced in this and well-equipped to manage those thoughts. The growth of God's word and power in your mind is beautiful.

Chapter 16

Seeking Wisdom

For the Lord *gives wisdom; from his mouth come knowledge and understanding.*
Proverbs 2:6 (NIV)

Over the years of raising children, there have been so many times I have looked at them and tried to give them advice to save them from the same mistakes that I have made. As I have watched this and reflected on my life, there are many times I have wished I had heeded the advice and wisdom of those who were older, which could have spared me mistakes.

Professionally, I have had the opportunity to spend a great deal of time with those who are older and wiser than I am. While I have received some advice over the years, I wish I had been more diligent in seeking out that wisdom more often. It is through life experiences and making mistakes that some of the best wisdom grows. By soliciting the advice of those who have had more life experiences, we can sometimes learn and avoid mistakes ourselves.

The Bible is full of wisdom written specifically to help us learn and to guide our steps. We can gain wisdom from God by reading his Word and by asking Him to grant us wisdom. James 1:5 tells us, "If any of you lacks wisdom, you should ask God, who gives generously to all without finding fault, and it will be given to you" (NIV).

In 2 Chronicles Chapter 1, we see the story of Solomon, who, in Verse 7, was approached by God, "That night God appeared to Solomon and said to him, 'Ask for whatever you want me to give you'" (NIV). In Verse 10, we see his request, "Give me wisdom and knowledge, that I may lead this people, for who is able to govern this great people of yours" (NIV)? As the chapter continues God grants this request, and Solomon becomes known as the wisest man who ever lived. His wisdom provided the contributions to the Bible by writing Proverbs, Ecclesiastes, and Song of Songs (Song of Solomon), known as the books of wisdom.

While our elders may carry a great deal of wisdom from their life experiences, and it can be valuable wisdom to seek, we ought to regularly seek the wisdom of our Father in heaven, who is the master of all wisdom. His wisdom is greater than any earthly wisdom and is described in James 3:17: "But the wisdom from above is first of all pure. It is also peace loving, gentle at all times, and willing to yield to others. It is full of mercy and the fruit of good deeds. It shows no favoritism and is always sincere" (NLT). His wisdom is readily available and will not lead us astray.

God offers continual access to wisdom that is always impartial and sincere when we seek the Lord's Word. So today if you need wisdom about a situation or a direction in your life, seek God and His Word, and He will provide. When you know the master of wisdom, who promises to grant it to us when you ask, you should never feel a lack of wisdom in your life. Wisdom is a powerful guide to your walk in life, preventing many pitfalls. So today may you seek the wisdom of our heavenly Father earnestly and often.

Chapter 17

Do It My Way

Seek his will in all you do, and he will show you which path to take.

Proverbs 3:6 (NLT)

When I was growing up, I had a tendency, as many kids do, to test my limits. I felt confident about the way I viewed things and, of course, thought I was much older, wiser, and more mature than I really was. Often this had the same ending. I found myself in a mess or in trouble. Then I did what most children do. I called my parents to bail me out or sought their advice to help.

I started this pattern at a very young age in my life. One day when I was three years old, a package came in the mail and I was determined to find out what was in it. As the story is told by my mother (because I was too young to remember), she was in the other room painting and told me to wait for her to open the package. I had a real need to see what was in it. The package had a plastic type string around it. So I got out a knife and went to work on trying to open it, only to slip with the knife and injure my eye. To this day, I am blind in that eye. This was the beginning of me trying to do things my way. Some might say it wasn't my fault at that age, but it demonstrates how I had a compulsion to go into things I decided to do with full force and little thought or planning. Over the years, I have learned to manage this part of my personality, but I also learned I need to seek the Lord for guidance in my life.

Sometimes, in our daily lives, we rush into things, and then once we are in them realize we should have sought God more before making the choices we made. The greatness and grandeur of the opportunity or adventure entices us to proceed without reservation. We just go full speed ahead then find ourselves in a struggle or with discontentment.

God knows we can have this tendency, and He guides us. We find in Psalm 32:8: "The Lord says, 'I will guide you along the best pathway for your life. I will advise you and watch over you" (NLT). God gives us all the answers and guidance we need for any circumstance or decision. However, we must seek His counsel before we move. It is when we move or make decisions without seeking Him first that we find ourselves like the child making a wrong turn, leading to harm, and then calling on the Lord to rescue us from the situation.

To avoid these types of situations, we must take time daily to seek God and follow the plans He has for us. Psalm 25:4-5 is the prayer each of us should pray daily: "Show me your ways, Lord, teach me your paths. Guide me in your truth and teach me, for you are God my Savior, and my hope is in you all day long" (NIV).

Today may you have a hope and trust in the Lord and patience in your steps, allowing you time to seek the Lord first. In seeking the Lord, may you keep yourself from situations where you find yourself calling out to the Lord for rescue. God always helps us when we make wrong steps or take wrong paths, but we can save ourselves much agony if we seek Him first. May your guidance be in the Lord that you may be on the right path, making the choices He is directing specifically for you.

Chapter 18

MVP Player

When pride comes, then comes disgrace, but with humility comes wisdom.
Proverbs 11:2 (NIV)

Years ago, there was a great football player (who will remain unnamed out of respect) who was named NFL MVP for a second time in his career. His second time he was co-named with another athlete. Instead of saying the customary statement about what an honor it was to get the award with this other outstanding football player, he declared he would have rather received the award solely for himself. From that day forward, I looked at this player through a different lens because of his lack of humility.

Years ago, my uncle, who was truly a man who lived and walked out his faith honorably, passed away. After the internment, my father commented to my aunt about how her sons had stepped up at this difficult time. He said, "You must be proud of them." My aunt quickly responded, telling us my uncle always said, "We Christians are to be humble and not prideful." He said that Christians could be well pleased with their children, but should not be proud since that was not being humble.

Scripture commands us repeatedly to be humble. Colossians 3:12 says, "Since God chose you to be the holy people he loves, you must clothe yourselves with tenderhearted mercy, kindness, humility, gentleness, and patience" (NLT). We also find in Ephesians 4:2, "Be completely humble and gentle" (NIV). James 4:10 says, "Humble yourself before the Lord and he will lift you up" (NIV). But not only does scripture tell us to be humble, it also clearly shows how much God hates pridefulness. James 4:6 says, "God opposes the proud but shows favor to the humble" (NIV).

As we strive to live our lives like Jesus, we must understand that even He humbled himself, even unto death. He could have been prideful about who his father was and His position with Him, but He was not. Philippians 2:6-8 says, "Who, being in very nature God, did not consider equality with God something to be used to his own advantage; rather, he made himself nothing by taking the very nature of a servant, being made in human likeness. And being found in appearance as a man, he humbled himself by becoming obedient to death—even death on a cross" (NIV). Jesus was in union with the Father in heaven, and yet He put that aside to become a human. Following God requires all of us to become humble.

Prideful people begin to believe they are better than others or the things they do or have are better. Oftentimes, pridefulness can lead to arrogance. Arrogance then leads to poor tolerance of criticism and makes it difficult to see others as superior to themselves. Hence why God has such a disdain for prideful people. Once filled with pride and arrogance, we no longer have the ability to honor God on the high place that He is seated. Lucifer himself became so prideful he wanted the honor and power of God alone. His pride caused him to be removed from heaven and forever known as Satan.

Dictionary.com tells us staying humble means to "know exactly your place, nothing more and nothing less." It also says a sense of humility comes by suppressing one's ego and sincerely taking somebody or something as it is, no judgment.

When we know our place in relation to our heavenly Father, we know He is great and mighty, and we are weak, fallible, insecure, and in need of Him. Remaining humble gives us the ability to have compassion for others. To have a strong faith and the protection of God, we must humble ourselves, recognizing our weakness and the greatness of our God. In knowing His greatness, we can have assurance of everything He is able to offer. Today may you continue to humble yourself that you may experience the ever-increasing greatness of God.

Chapter 19

Hand Hygiene

Wash me clean from my guilt. Purify me from my sin.
Psalm 51:2 (NLT)

Over the years I have seen technology evolve and change healthcare in innumerable ways to improve patient care. However, one thing that has not changed over all these years is hand hygiene. The simple act of washing our hands remains a cornerstone in infection prevention. As diseases have become more communicable and rampant over the years, infection prevention has become increasingly important, yet compliance within healthcare remains an ongoing struggle for any organization. Healthcare facilities are continually searching for varying approaches to improve compliance because the benefits of consistent and regular cleaning of hands is so vital to disease control. Proper cleansing and the use of protection when exposed to germs is essential to preventing workers and others from contracting illnesses.

We also have a spiritual hygiene. This is in relation to how clean we are in our lives. We should ask ourselves, "Are we taking steps to ensure we remain spiritually clean?" Just like germs have a way of infecting those who are not using good hand hygiene, the enemy and things of this world can infect us spiritually and cause us to have a sickened spiritual life when we do not practice good spiritual hygiene.

James 4:8 says, "Come close to God, and God will come close to you. Wash your hands, you sinners; purify your hearts, for your loyalty is divided between God and the world" (NLT). Ezekiel 36:25 says, "I will sprinkle clean water on you, and you will be clean; I will cleanse you from all your impurities and from all your idols" (NIV). And Isaiah 1:16 says, "Wash yourselves; make yourselves clean; remove the evil of your deeds from before my eyes; cease to do evil" (ESV).

Being spiritually clean, just like hand hygiene, can be very simple to understand yet very difficult to remain compliant. Having a strong faith requires regular examination of ourselves and our lives to determine our spiritual hygiene. How clean are we keeping ourselves? Are we regularly cleansing ourselves when we are not spiritually clean? Just like we need to use gowns and goggles to supplement hand hygiene in healthcare, ensuring we are limiting our exposures, we must also look for ways to protect us spiritually. By the nature of our job, nurses know we are going to be exposed to germs and illnesses regularly that can make us unhealthy, and the same is true in our spiritual lives.

Good spiritual hygiene remains essential to keeping your faith walk healthy. So today I encourage you to purify yourself from any evil and uncleanliness in your life. May your faith be strong and healthy, and may you delight in good spiritual hygiene.

Chapter 20

Let Freedom Ring

So if the Son sets you free, you will be free indeed.
John 8:36 (NIV).

The Statue of Liberty is a symbol held dear by Americans. It was given to the United States as a gift from France to honor the United States and commemorate the centennial of the Declaration of Independence. It is a figure of the Roman liberty goddess holding a torch above her head with her right hand. In her left hand she holds a tablet with the date the US Declaration of Independence was signed. It is a representation of our freedom and is visited by many Americans each year.

Liberty is a founding value of our country. Our Pledge of Allegiance concludes with, "...one nation under God indivisible with liberty and justice for all." Dictionary Online defines liberty as, "the state of being free within society from oppressive restrictions imposed by authority on one's way of life, behavior, or political views." Wikipedia describes liberty in theology as "freedom from the effects of sin, spiritual servitude, or worldly ties."

Scripture repeatedly tells us about the freedom we receive through Christ as we walk in our Christian faith. The Statue of Liberty reminds us that freedom comes at a price. Our freedom in faith also came at a price, the death of Jesus Christ. This cross is the symbolic reminder of our freedom. This privilege in faith grants us the freedom from sin and oppression by the enemy.

As citizens of the United States, we have obligations to uphold the liberty we have in this country. As Christians, while we didn't have to purchase or earn our own liberty, God does give us responsibilities as part of that freedom. Galatians 5:13 says, "For you have been called to live in freedom, my brothers and sisters. But don't use your freedom to satisfy your sinful nature. Instead, use your freedom to serve one another in love" (NLT). Galatians 5:1 says, "So Christ has truly set us free. Now make sure that you stay free, and don't get tied up again in slavery to the law" (NLT). And James 1:25 says, "But whoever looks intently into the perfect law that gives freedom, and continues in it—not forgetting what they have heard, but doing it—they will be blessed in what they do" (NIV).

As we embrace our freedom in faith, we need to honor God by never allowing our sinful nature to rob us of it. We need to witness to the world the peace, hope and joy that comes from being free in faith. We must be a representation of what it looks like to live in religious freedom given to us by our Savior.

When we look at the Statue of Liberty, we are reminded of the liberty in this country, the price paid for it, and the responsibility to preserve it. The same is how we ought to look at our liberty in Christ. We must recognize there was a huge price paid for it and there is a responsibility to live a life of Christian freedom.

Today praise the Lord for liberating us and show your gratitude in the demonstration of how you live your life. May you daily reflect on the liberty you have received by persevering against the slavery of sin and the enemy.

Chapter 21

Great Opportunities

Because he bends down to listen, I will pray as long as I have breath!
Psalm 116:2 (NLT)

Part of living is searching for the best opportunities. We look for great opportunities in our education, career, children, vacations, and the list goes on. We search what will give us the most out of each of those opportunities. When we miss a great opportunity, we are left with frustration and sometimes upset to varying degrees, depending on what that opportunity may have offered. We can also miss prayer opportunities when we are not tuned into the Lord and miss chances to lift others up in prayer.

As a nurse practitioner, I took care of a married couple, both individually and jointly. At one point, they were struggling with substantial health problems that would mean the husband, who was the breadwinner, might not be able to return to his job. They were faced with overwhelming decisions about their health and finances. They were deciding whether they should move back to their home state and how the cost of doing this would affect them long-term.

One day when they came into the office, they were particularly struggling. I came into the exam room and was about to proceed with my routine when they stopped me and said, "Before you do anything, will you just pray for us?" This was a memorable visit because I worked for an organization that was not faith-based and speaking too freely in my job could pose a threat to my job. But their request opened the door to a faith conversation and provided me with a gift of being able to pray for them. We shared a very powerful moment that day.

To this day, I have maintained a close relationship with this couple, even though I haven't seen them in years. On special days I will get messages from them, and when they are struggling they will request me to pray for them. I treasure this experience with them and the relationship we developed. However, it does make me wonder how many missed opportunities for prayer with patients have happened over the years. Opportunities where the person may have desperately needed prayer but was not as bold as this couple to request that from their medical provider.

In the Old Testament, there was a tabernacle with three curtains. The first curtain was at the gate of the entrance into the tabernacle—it separated the people from the outer court of the tabernacle. The second was to gain entrance into the Holy place where only priests were allowed. Finally, the third curtain allowed entrance into the Holy of Holies, which contained the Ark of the Covenant and God's presence could be experienced. Only the high priest was allowed to enter the Holy of Holies and only once a year. The priest at this time was to bring offerings before the Lord along with the prayers of all the people.

This veil in the temple that was the barrier to the Holy of

Holies was torn from bottom to top when Jesus died on the cross. Removal of this barrier provided freedom for all of us to be able to come before the Lord. This means regardless of the day, our location, our church status, or position, we can freely come boldly to the throne of the Lord. We have the opportunity to come to the Lord, which prior to Jesus's death and resurrection was reserved only for the High Priests. Today we can freely come to the Lord bringing prayers and praises.

In Ephesians 6:18, it says, "Pray in the Spirit at all times and on every occasion. Stay alert and be persistent in your prayers for all believers everywhere" (NLT). There is a blessing for the individual being prayed for but an even greater one for the person bringing prayer on someone's behalf. Galatians 6:2 says, "Carry each other's burdens, and in this way you will fulfill the law of Christ"(NIV). And James 5:16 says, "Confess your sins to each other and pray for each other so that you may be healed. The earnest prayer of a righteous person has great power and produces wonderful results"(NLT).

What a special privilege that has been granted by the Lord that we can come before Him with prayer any day and at any time. Today and every day of your life we get the opportunity to come before the Lord and lift others up in prayer.

So today may you have eyes to see prayer opportunities around you and the faithfulness to seize those opportunities that you may fulfill the law of Christ. Today may you stay alert embracing daily opportunities to be the righteous person producing great power and wonderful results from the Lord because of your prayers. May you not have any missed prayer opportunities.

Chapter 22

Limitless

Look, God is greater than we can understand. His years cannot be counted.
Job 36:26 (NLT)

Over the years, I have had to learn many lessons the hard way. One of these is to say "no". "No" is a two-letter word that can be a struggle to say. In the past, I have found myself volunteering to help at church, at my children's school, and with their extracurricular activities. I have said yes to being on committees in the community or special committees at work in addition to my full-time job. I have learned that when I get involved in so many things, I can become overwhelmed and drained. Yet when asked to do something extra, I am wrought with the guilt of saying, "No." Sometimes we forget how much we can handle and that we indeed have limitations. Having too many things to do can result in us not taking care of ourselves. We start sleeping less, stop exercising, and stop taking time to spend with the Lord or reading the Bible. I have been in this position, and it is exhausting.

During my days in graduate school, I was working part time, raising three children, my husband and I were doing foster care, and I was president of our children's swim club. My days were filled with stress and concern for how I would get everything done. I drank coffee most of the day to have enough energy to get through and ate a terrible diet. I did not exercise regularly, if at all, and spent little to no extra time with the Lord. This led me to a place of exhaustion, fatigue, irritability, obesity, sleep deprivation, and spiritual emptiness. This period in my life was a profound lesson in the value of understanding my limits and having the grace to allow myself to say no even to really good things.

However, the beauty of our Father in heaven is that He has no limits. We can be fully assured He is a limitless God. Jeremiah 32:27 says, "I am the Lord, the God of all the peoples of the world. Is anything too hard for me?" (NIV). Throughout scripture, we are told nothing is too difficult for our Lord. This is described in Jeremiah 32:17 where it says, "O Sovereign Lord! You made the heavens and earth by your strong hand and powerful arm. Nothing is too hard for You!" (NLT). Matthew 19:26 also emphasizes this saying, "But Jesus looked at them and said, 'With man this is impossible, but with God all things are possible'" (ESV).

As I have traveled, I have seen great oceans with water beyond what the eye can view. I have seen towering mountains that seem to reach up to the sky. I have seen the Grand Canyon and its vastness. All these display the greatness of creation made by our Lord, demonstrating the limitlessness of our God.

Today remember that "No" is an okay word for us to use because as human beings our abilities are limited. Be reassured that when we need to say no, God will ensure there is someone to fill the gap as He works all things out. The God we know and worship is never overwhelmed, burdened, or drained. He is limitless. Because our God has no limits, we can look at any situation with confidence, knowing it will never be bigger than our Father.

Chapter 23

Bible Meditation

May these words of my mouth and this meditation of my heart be pleasing in your sight, LORD, my Rock and my Redeemer.
Psalm 19:14 (NIV)

Some people describe me as being a little "high-strung". I have been in meetings and classes where they encourage a brief period of meditation prior to beginning, allowing your mind to be in the right state. This has always been a challenge for me; quieting my mind and relaxing are not something I do easily.

However, meditation has become very popular over the years. It is frequently used to help reduce stress and anxiety and aid in relaxation. The practice of meditation is thousands of years old and was originally derived from the ancient world, stemming from philosophies and religions. Mayoclinic.com describes meditation as "a type of mind-body complementary medicine. Meditation can produce a deep state of relaxation and a tranquil mind. During meditation, you focus your attention and eliminate the stream of jumbled thoughts that may be crowding your mind and causing stress."

Wikipedia says, "Meditation is a technique to train attention and awareness and achieve a mentally clear and emotionally calm and stable state." It is when we are able to meditate and get into God's presence that we can be in a God-mind state. It is where the stream of thoughts crowding our minds is silenced and the Lord can have our full attention, clarity, and emotional availability, allowing us to clearly hear Him and absorb the words He has for us.

In our walk with Christ, meditation can be a type of contemplative prayer that creates a sense of union with God. Meditation is not something New Age, but something age-old found in scripture. Scripture stresses the need to have meditation as part of our Christian practices. Joshua 1:8 says, "Keep this Book of the law always on your lips; meditate on it day and night, so that you may be careful to do everything written in it. Then you will be prosperous and successful" (NIV). Psalm 1:1-2 also says, "Blessed is the one who does not walk in step with the wicked or stand in the way that sinners take or sit in the company of mockers, but whose delight is in the law of the LORD, and who meditates on his law day and night" (NIV).

Meditation on His Word will allow you to know and understand His ways, truths, and commands. Through this meditation, you will obtain mental clarity and emotional calm that can come only from the Lord. You will be able to gain a complete awareness of the Lord and His power, love, and purpose.

Today may you spend time in meditation with God, allowing you to experience mental clarity, calmness, and stability. May you be able to clearly hear Him because of the time you dedicate to being in His presence. May meditation on God and His Word become part of your relationship building with the Savior.

Chapter 24

Matter of Perspective

All praise to God, the Father of our Lord Jesus Christ. It is by his great mercy that we have been born again, because God raised Jesus Christ from the dead. Now we live with great expectation, and we have a priceless inheritance- an inheritance that is kept in heaven for you, pure and undefiled, beyond the reach of change and decay.

1 Peter 1:3-4 (NLT)

My oldest son and I have very different political beliefs. We each have our reasons we believe we are right. We look at the government and politics with opposing opinions, being from different generations and having separate issues that are important to us. We see things through very different lenses and tend to be passionate about the lens we are looking through. We have very different perspectives on the topics and issues.

Perspectives can vary widely. Merriam-Webster has multiple definitions for perspective, but one is: "the capacity to view things in their true relations or relative importance."

Regardless of our perspectives on things in life, as Christians, there is one identical perspective we should all have—that is an eternal perspective. Having this mindset is key to living as a true Christian. An eternal perspective is one where our focus is not on earthly things and concerns but on godly and heavenly concerns.

This world drives us to focus on things in the here and now, making our time on earth difficult. It can easily tear us down and destroy us unless we are able to "see the bigger picture" to know what God has in eternity. When our eyes are on things above and our perspective is eternal, we are more able to manage and cope with the things of this world.

Having an eternal perspective helps us to keep our lives centered on God and the things of heaven. A mindset on things above will affect the choices we make and the priorities we have in our lives. This type of focus changes how we approach things in our lives and how we see pain, pleasure and purpose. An eternal perspective can change how we live, how we view challenges, and how we treat others.

Without an eternal perspective, we misinterpret things in our lives. We fuel unhealthy feelings and negative energy, which serves no purpose other than to bring us down. Maintaining an eternal perspective allows us to view things differently and changes our priorities, bringing us closer to the Lord and giving us more peace. Colossians 3:1-2 says, "Since you have been raised to new life with Christ, set your sights on the realities of heaven, where Christ sits in the place of honor at God's right hand. Think about the things of heaven, not the things of earth" (NLT). Today may your perspective be eternal praising God.

Chapter 25

Church Etiquette

But if anyone has the world's goods and sees his brother in need, yet closes his heart against him, how does God's love abide in him?

1 John 3:17 (ESV)

There was a story years ago in one of the papers in North Dakota where a man went into a Catholic church and was found bathing in a holy water font. This story first made the local news and eventually made it to national television, perceived as humorous. As I heard this, I was greatly saddened because this man likely was homeless and even more likely had some degree of mental illness. The publicity of this event demonstrated he was treated with criticism and ridiculed rather than with love and warmth by the church.

In John Chapter 12 we see people astounded over the actions of one woman, named Mary, at a particular dinner. This was a dinner given in Jesus's honor at His friends' home, where Mary proceeded to wash the feet of Jesus. We do not know how the woman knew about Jesus, but she revered Him so much that she wanted to approach Him where he was sitting to pay honor to Him. It was uncustomary and against the culture to approach a man at the table and wash his feet. In addition, in Jewish culture at this time, a woman was not allowed to even touch a rabbi like Jesus.

In the first century, people would not have sat at a table without washing their feet. The tables used in those days were very low, and people sat on pillows on the floor. Because of the way they would need to position their feet, they would be very near the table and the person sitting beside you. Cleansing of feet became very desirable since walking was the main means of transportation in those days. People walked in the desert sand with sandals, causing the feet to get very dusty and dirty and making the practice of washing feet essential. If a host were to omit the practice of washing of feet, it would be seen as marked unfriendliness. Washing feet was not something unique in this story; it was a standard of daily living and a sign of being a good host.

This woman used an expensive perfume, one that would have been equivalent to a year's wages, to wash the feet of Jesus. Then she took down her hair, which was also not socially acceptable to do in public, to wipe His feet. As this was happening, Judas (one of the disciples) objected and asked why this expensive perfume was not being sold and the money given to the poor. Judas, who would later betray Jesus, was the treasurer or keeper of the money for Jesus and the disciples. Scripture tells us that Judas was a thief and would pilfer some of this money, so in this situation he only saw money being lost. But Jesus defended Mary and said, "Leave her alone, so that she may keep it (the rest of the perfume) for the day of my burial" (John 12:7 ESV).

This was a gathering of people seeking Jesus, where she

should have felt safe and free from rejection in honoring the Lord. Yet, despite being among the disciples and Jesus, someone questioned her actions and how she was honoring Him. It can be easy, even within the walls of the church where people ought to be safe, to find ourselves looking at others with a critical eye and judgment, as Judas did.

Ephesians describes the responsibilities of the church, saying, "Now these are the gifts Christ gave to the church: the apostles, the prophets, the evangelists, and the pastors and teachers. Their responsibility is to equip God's people to do his work and build up the church, the body of Christ. This will continue until we all come to such unity in our faith and knowledge of God's Son that we will be mature in the Lord, measuring up to the full and complete standard of Christ" (Ephesians 4:11-13 NLT). We are to lift up those around us and encourage them in the Lord.

Today may our eyes be like those of Jesus and see the needs of people versus noticing the way they are not following the social norm. May we especially have those eyes within the church, making it a safe place for all regardless of their societal standing. May we, as Christians, see the needs and hurt of people over the ability to see how they deviate from societal expectations. God calls all of us His children without any criteria or prerequisites.

Chapter 26

Holistic Spirituality

Let the message about Christ, in all its richness, fill your lives. Teach and counsel each other with all the wisdom he gives. Sing psalms hymns and spiritual songs to God with thankful hearts.

Colossians 3:16 (NLT)

As part of my professional continuing education, I once attended a conference entirely dedicated to holistic health. Holistic health addresses the physical, mental, emotional, social, and spiritual components of health using various disciplines not traditionally used in medicine, including religious and cultural practices to heal people. These practices are designed to be used in addition to or instead of traditional Western medical practices. One conference speaker stated the United States outspends all other countries in healthcare and yet ranks fiftieth in life expectancy. The American healthcare system is designed primarily to diagnose and treat illness, with much less time and money spent on prevention and health promotion. Attention is primarily spent on treatment and management of diseases and disorders ailing our population.

This conference left me wondering about spiritual health. Is our faith like the healthcare of the United States? Do we seek God only in times of crisis? When things are going wrong or times of being "ill"? Or are we seeking him to build our faith, know him better, and provide strength for times of trouble? God assures us that He will rescue his children regardless of what situations occur in our lives. Psalm 46:1 reminds us of this: "God is our refuge and strength, a very present help in trouble" (ESV). Matthew 11:28 says, "Come to me, all you who are weary and burdened, and I will give you rest" (NIV). God does not put conditions on the promises that He will be there for us at all times as long as we belong to him. Yet how much better would our spiritual health be if we took a more holistic approach and used all the resources God gives us to build our faith and walk closer to Him prior to any crisis. People who pursue preventive health find themselves sick less often and are better able to recover when they become ill. When we are spiritually healthy, we can face circumstances with more confidence and less worry and are not robbed of our hope.

When we seek God daily, our spiritual health becomes vibrant, alive, and energized. I often teach my patients about things they can do to help stay healthy. Regarding their diet, I tell them, "You can't drive your car without fuel. Your body can't run without fuel either." The same thing is true in our faith. We can't have a "well running" strong faith without regularly fueling it. First John 2:6 says, "Whoever claims to live in him must live as Jesus did" (NIV). Jesus regularly spent time with His Father.

One excuse people will make to build their spiritual health is they do not have enough time. There has never been and never will be anyone who had more to do than Jesus, yet He always made time to spend with His Father. So having a busy schedule should never be an excuse for our leniency with time spent with the Lord. Jesus always made spending time with God a top priority. He would leave large crowds wanting more time with Him just to be with His Father. We need to mimic this in our lives.

In order to have a strong, holistic spiritual health, you need time with God regularly and frequently. As you care for your spiritual health, may you find a strong faith regardless of calm or crisis in your life. May you fuel your faith that it may be strong within you.

Chapter 27

Auditory Assessment

For merely listening to the law doesn't make us right with God.
It is obeying the law that makes us right in his sight.
Romans 2:13 (NLT)

Doing annual physical exams is a part of my work as a nurse practitioner. When it comes to assessing people's hearing, I often ask, "How is your hearing?" If it's a child and I have a parent in the room or a patient with a spouse with them, it is not uncommon for them to speak up and make some comment, usually about poor hearing. I tend to quickly respond saying, "Hearing and listening are two very different things." I am referring to the patient's actual physical ability to use their senses and hear sounds. The family member making the derogatory comment is usually referring to the ability to follow instructions or do something as a result of what is said.

Scripture says in Matthew 11:15, "Anyone with ears to hear should listen and understand!" (NLT). Many of us, myself included, like to talk, and it's not that we don't like to listen, we just feel we have a lot to say. The act of listening to God is vital in our faith walk.

Scripture gives us many reasons that listening is important. Romans 10:17 says, "So faith comes from hearing, that is, hearing the Good News about Christ" (NLT). Hebrews 3:7-8 says, "Therefore, as the Holy Spirit says, 'Today if you hear his voice, do not harden your hearts'"(ESV), and Isaiah 55:10-11 says, "For as the rain and the snow come down from heaven and do not return there but water the earth, making it bring forth and sprout, giving seed to the sower and bread to the eater, so shall my word be that goes out from my mouth; it shall not return to me empty, but it shall accomplish that which I purpose, and shall succeed in the thing for which I sent it" (ESV).

Listening to God requires us to actively engage in time and conversation with Him. Conversation with God is not a speech-centered conversation like we are accustomed to with people. However, in this century, we have conversations all the time without actually speaking. We have conversations via voicemails, emails, and texting. A conversation with God is one where we are engaging through thoughts and prayers. God then responds by revealing things to us through scripture and the Holy Spirit within us. Being sensitive to the Holy Spirit allows us to fully understand the words he offers.

Hearing is vital to knowing God, but listening is how we develop a relationship with Him and how we receive His blessings. God will speak to us in many ways, requiring us to learn to listen in whichever way He is speaking. We ought never just hear God speak, but we must listen. Luke 8:15 tells us, "As for that in the good soil, they are those who, hearing the word, hold it fast in an honest and good heart, and bear fruit with patience" (NLT).

Today may the Lord know that not only did you hear His

word and Him speak, but that you also listened. May you find in listening to the Lord you are doing His work. As you listen to Him, you will find the right directions in your life, answers to situations, and a contentment knowing your life is directed by the Lord.

Chapter 28

Amputation Option

He cuts off every branch of mine that doesn't produce fruit, and he prunes the branches that do bear fruit so they will produce even more.
John 15:2 (NLT)

Some patients with chronic medical problems affecting their circulation can develop infections and open wounds in the lower extremities. When these wounds become severely infected or the tissues start to die, becoming necrotic (dead), they may be faced with amputation. Once an infected or necrotic tissue is progressing and not responding to treatment, it begins to affect the rest of the body. The body struggles to survive and thrive in the midst of a disease that is robbing the rest of the healthy body of nutrients and begins to poison the entire person.

When we choose to start walking in faith, there are things we need to leave behind. These are the things that distract us and cause us to sin. We oftentimes can recognize the need to remove these things from our lives and are ready to give them up when we become new believers. There is an excitement and momentum that comes with this exciting step into the faith journey. But once the newness of this change wears off or the enemy throws trials and tribulations in our path, we begin to struggle with keeping those things out of our lives.

In the story of David and Goliath, we know that, with a sling and rock, David was able to defeat this giant of a man who was dressed in full armor. But there is another part of the story that is important. After Goliath was defeated and lay dead on the ground, David took Goliath's sword and cut off his head (1 Samuel 17:51). Beheading is known as the ultimate life-extinguishing act. This can be symbolic for us in relation to extinguishing certain thoughts, actions, and behaviors in our lives. We need to be able to cut off those things that drive our actions and behaviors to deviate from Christ.

We need to develop a practice of recognizing the things that are leading us astray and are causing us to be tempted by sin and the ways of the world. Matthew 5:30 says, "And if your right hand causes you to stumble, cut it off and throw it away. It is better for you to lose one part of your body than for your whole body to go into hell" (NIV). Cutting off things of sin in our lives will free us. Just as the necrotic dying tissue of an ill person can begin killing the rest of the body, the same thing will happen to us spiritually when we entertain these unhealthy thoughts and actions. They will cause us spiritual decline.

The enemy, Satan, uses his power to sneak into our minds and put thoughts that are spiritually unhealthy. Having the Holy Spirit within us gives us a power that can overcome any power or thoughts Satan will try to use as temptation. We can empower ourselves and make a statement to Satan that he ought to fear the power we have within us. When we are able to cut these thoughts off, it tells him these things are completely dead to us, cannot and will not interject into our lives causing us to sidestep or be led astray in our faith walk.

Today may you have victory as you cut things off by the head that are spiritually unhealthy. May there be finality to the power these thoughts have in your life. Cutting off the head is a powerful symbolism that ought to remind you how to permanently rid these things from your life so you can walk more abundantly in the faith of God.

Chapter 29

Where's Your Shield

The LORD will keep you from all harm- he will watch over your life;
Psalm 121:7 (NIV)

I am a fan of action movies, whether they be military-based, a superhero rescuing someone through an impossible mission, or a Western. One of the things that always happens in the heat of these battles, when bullets are flying and danger is all around them, is the need to seek shelter. Shelter is a basic human need and provides protection and a barrier from the elements or circumstances. Throughout scripture we are told about the protection God offers us.

Psalm 91 is a powerful psalm that is known as a psalm to pray for protection. It is often invoked in times of trouble and hardship. Verse 3 says, "Surely he will save you from the fowler's snare and from the deadly pestilence" (NIV), and Verse 4 says, "He will cover you with his feathers, and under his wings you will find refuge; his faithfulness will be your shield and rampart" (NIV). In the English Standard Version, the translators say His faithfulness is "a shield and buckler," and in the New Living Translation His faithfulness promises an "armor and protection". The imagery of a shield from the Lord, needed for protection is echoed in Ephesians 6: 10-18, where we are told to put on the full armor of God. Verse 16 it, "In addition to all of these (referring to the other parts of the armor cited in previous verses), hold up the shield of faith to stop the fiery arrows of the devil" (NLT).

During biblical times and the days of Roman soldiers, the shield was instrumental in providing protection. Shields originated from pieces of tree bark, wood, or stretched animal skin. The metal shield was not available until smelting was discovered and refined. Once metal shields originated, they evolved into many kinds, depending on the needs of that soldier and their situation. Some were long and covered the entire body, some were short and were used only when specific parts of the body needed to be protected. The ideal shield was large enough to give complete protection, not too heavy and yet small enough to easily handle, while protecting the parts of the body that were in danger (womeninthebible.net).

Regardless of the type of shield used, they often provided protection for the chest area, over the heart. The metal shield is referenced throughout scripture. In Ephesians, the shield is described as a protection from the fiery arrow of the devil. The shield protects the heart, and the devil does not target a finger, toe, arm, or leg—he wants to get at our heart.

God understands the attack the enemy has on our heart, necessitating a shield. The stronger our faith, the better our shield and the more protection it will provide. Weakness in our faith leaves us unprotected and vulnerable to the attacks of the enemy. His attacks will try to diminish faith by luring us into strongholds and things in our lives that distract us from building our faith.

Today if you are struggling to stay strong in your faith, I encourage you to recognize the need to seek ways to build up that faith providing full protection. With that protection, the enemy cannot access your heart and will be rendered useless in his attacks. Then when attacks come despite wearing your armor, know that your Lord is standing there to enhance your shield and to be your refuge and fortress and will cover you with his feathers and allow you to rest under his wings (Psalm 91:2-4). Today may your faith be strong and your protection be complete.

Chapter 30

Death Departure

Don't be so surprised! Indeed, the time is coming when all the dead in their graves will hear the voice of God's Son, and they will rise again. Those who have done good will rise to experience eternal life, and those who have continued in evil will rise to experience judgment.
John 5:28-29 (NLT)

Working in hospice and oncology, we regularly face patients with a poor prognosis. As we provide health care for these patients, we frequently have conversations with patients and their family about dying. Each of us can recall varying experiences and conversations with people that are near death or in actually witnessing a death.

I vividly remember one conversation with a nurse who had the opportunity to be with a woman as she was in her dying days and through her final breath. These moments can be an incredible opportunity when we know the person is close to the Lord and will soon be at the magnificent feet of Jesus. There is a reassurance we can give a family as they are grieving about the victory their loved one will soon obtain in their death. However, in this particular situation, the nurse, who was a strong Christian, said to me it was a difficult death because she was not sure the patient knew the Lord. She went on to tell me how the family said at the time of death, "At least she was not suffering anymore." The nurse said to me, "I pray she went to heaven and her misery was truly over and not just beginning."

Death is decision day, and it can be glorious or it can be the start of misery. In my own experience, I have been with both believing and nonbelievers in their death. These experiences can be very different. It is always a gut-wrenching experience with a nonbeliever, knowing there is no more time to change their minds. They made their decision about whether they would accept Christ or not.

Scripture warns us of the circumstances we will encounter in hell if we do not choose to follow God. Matthew 13:42 describes hell as a "blazing furnace, where there will be weeping and gnashing of teeth" (NIV). Second Thessalonians 1:9 says, "They will be punished with eternal destruction, forever separated from the Lord and from his glorious power" (NLV). And Matthew 25:46 says, "Then they will go away to eternal punishment, but the righteous to eternal life" (NIV).

The Lord loves all His dear children and is waiting for all of us. He says in Revelation 3:20, "Behold, I stand at the door and knock. If anyone hears My voice and opens the door, I will come in to him and eat with him, and he with me" (ESV). He is knocking at the door of our lives, continually waiting for an invitation to enter. God is patient in His waiting for us. 2 Peter 3:9 says, "The Lord is not slow in keeping his promise, as some understand slowness. Instead he is patient with you, not wanting anyone to perish, but everyone to come to repentance" (NIV). He does not have a time limit during our lives on our opportunity to come to Him. But that time limit expires at the time of our death.

You alone know where you are in your faith journey and salvation. If you have not opened the door the Lord is knocking on in your life, I encourage you to open that door now. Let the Lord into your life, and you will experience greatness beyond anything you could imagine. I encourage you today to ensure your destiny in the Lord. We have a Savior who gladly opens His arms and receives each one of us when we come to Him. When you know the Lord and follow Him, you can be assured every day that "The steadfast love of the LORD never ceases; his mercies never come to an end; they are new every morning" (Lamentations 3:22-23 ESV). Let the love of the Lord and His mercies shower you every day on this earth and in the destiny to come in eternity.

Prayer of Salvation

If you have never prayed the prayer of salvation and asked the Lord into your heart, I encourage you to pray the prayer below and see your life change. We at Pursuing Christ Ministries are here to help you on that faith journey, so please visit our website at Pursuingchristministries.org. for more information.

Jesus,

I believe that you are the only begotten Son of God and came to earth to be the Savior of the world, and that by Your death on the cross, You paid the price for the sin of the world so that whoever believes in You would not perish but have everlasting life.

I accept Your death as the penalty for my sin. I confess my sins and ask for Your forgiveness. cleanse me and make me Your child. I invite You into my heart and receive You as my Lord and Savior. My past has been erased from the record, and all the things have become new. I now receive Your Holy Spirit, who promised to never leave me. Fill me with new desires that honor You, and help me to become the person You want me to be.

In Your Name.

Amen

About The Author

Tamala May, a Christian author and speaker, built a career by serving others in the healthcare industry. After twenty-one years of serving God in this role, she found herself amid a deep personal crisis that led to a brokenness she had never known before. As a result, she sought the Lord and found new depths of faith and conviction. She began to lead Bible studies and encourage others in their daily spiritual walk. Over time, she discovered an anointing from God and began writing messages that she received from God. She has surrendered to this calling and is now publishing these devotions to inspire others in their faith journey. She continues to work as a Nurse Practitioner and is the mother of three children and a grandmother.

Books by Tamala May

Starting The Journey
Find comfort and support in this 30-Day Devotional.

Overcoming When It Hurts
Understanding your pain through people in the Bible.

Made in the USA
Columbia, SC
07 February 2025